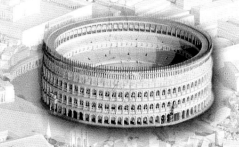

IMPERIAL R

AND THE ST. PETER'S BASILICA

INCLUDING TRANSPARENT OVERLAYS OF
ANCIENT ROME - POMPEII - VILLA ADRIANA

LOZZI ROMA - MILLENIUM

© LOZZI ROMA s.a.s. - MILLENIUM s.r.l.

ROMA IMPERIALE

Editore *(Publisher)*:

LOZZI ROMA s.a.s.

Via Filippo Nicolai, 91 - 00136 Roma
Tel. 06 35497051 - Fax 06 35497074
E-mail: lozziroma@tiscalinet.it - Web: www.lozziroma.com

Coeditore *(Co-publisher)*:

EDIZIONI MILLENIUM s.r.l.

Via della Magliana, 74 /e - 00100 Roma
Tel. 06 55286146
E-mail: atmercu@tin.it - Web: www.romagift.it

Fotolito:
TIPOCROM s.r.l. - Roma

Stampa:
Arti Grafiche Barlocchi - Settimo Milanese (Milano)

I disegni sono stati realizzati da Andrea Tosolini

Fotografie:
Archivio fotografico LOZZI ROMA s.a.s.
L'immagine a pag. 25 è stata gentilmente concessa dalla Sopraintendenza Archeologica di Roma.
Le immagini alle pagine 82, 83 e 87 sono state gentilmente concesse dall'Ufficio fotografico della Reverenda Fabbrica di San Pietro.
L'immagine a pagina 86 è stata gentilmente concessa dall'Ufficio fotografico dell'Osservatore Romano.
I plastici della Roma Imperiale, di A. Gismondi, sono tutti conservati presso il Museo della Civiltà Romana, EUR - Roma.

Gladiatorial combat in the arena of the Colosseum. ⇨

HISTORY OF ANCIENT ROME

According to legend, Rome was founded in **753 BC**, when **Romulus**, its first king, traced a furrow in the earth to mark the boundaries of the city. Romulus was succeeded by six kings: The Sabine **Numa Pompilius** (715 BC - 673 BC); the Roman **Tullus Hostilius** (673 BC - 642 BC) under whom the city of Alba Longa was defeated; **Ancus Marcius** (641 BC - 617 BC); **Tarquinius Priscus** (616 BC - 579 BC), of Etruscan origin, like the Tarquins which followed, built projects like the Circus Maximus, the Cloaca Maxima and the Mammertine Prison; **Servius Tullius** (578 BC - 534 BC), contributed to the growth of the city

Roman currency with the figure of Octavian Augustus.

through reforms of state institutions, the construction of an aqueduct and an imposing wall surrounding the city (the Servian Wall). The tyranny of the last king, **Tarquinius "the Superb"**, led the Roman people to overthrow the monarchy and establish the Roman Republic (509 BC).

The urban growth of Rome under the monarchy was accompanied by a notable increase in the population, which by 500 BC had reached nearly 15,000 for the 100 square-kilometer area. Rome had by then become an important political center, adorned by public works of notable artistic value; the Forum was paved and the Temple of Jupiter rose on the Capital Hill.

Under the monarchy the social order had been

Small model of a Roman biga.

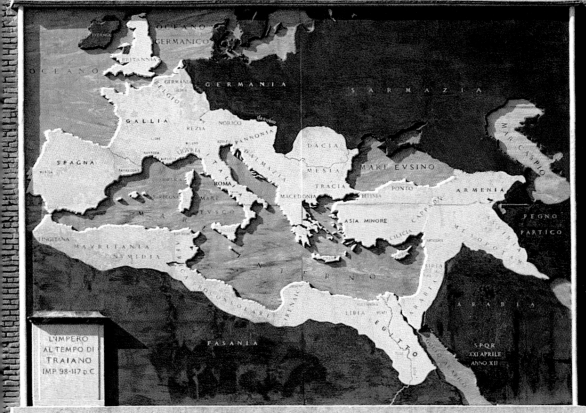

L'IMPERO
AL TEMPO DI
TRAIANO
IMP. 98-117 p.C.

117 AD - THE ROMAN EMPIRE AT ITS GREATEST EXTENT.

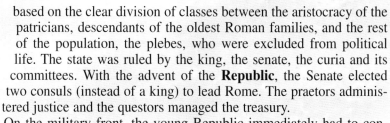

based on the clear division of classes between the aristocracy of the patricians, descendants of the oldest Roman families, and the rest of the population, the plebes, who were excluded from political life. The state was ruled by the king, the senate, the curia and its committees. With the advent of the **Republic**, the Senate elected two consuls (instead of a king) to lead Rome. The praetors administered justice and the questors managed the treasury.

On the military front, the young Republic immediately had to confront threats from the Etruscans and went to war against the Latin League, which did not tolerate Roman territorial supremacy. But already by the end of the 6th century BC, Rome dominated Lazio and the area south of the Tiber.

In 390 BC, Rome **was invaded by the Gauls**, whose victory favored the rise, however short-lived, of other Italic peoples. The mid-4th century BC saw a large Roman expansion into Central-Southern Italy. When the Romans took control of the Magnagrecia (further south), they could no longer ignore the Mediterranean power of Carthage.

In 264 BC, under the pretext of the control of Eastern Sicily, Rome and Carthage fought what was to be the **First Punic War**. A strong Roman navy ensured victory in 241 BC. With the peace treaty Rome annexed Sicily, and later Sardinia and Corsica.

In 222 BC, the Roman legions put an end to the incursions of the Gauls and Ligurians, which had begun six years earlier. This military success greatly enlarged the Roman territory into the Po valley.

Marcus Aurelius.   *Model of the Roman Forum between the Campidoglio and the Colosseum.*

Helmet used by gladiators.

Gold coin with the profile of the Emperor Tiberius.

In 218 BC **Hannibal** led the Carthaginian armies to Italy through Spain, crossing the Pyranees and the Alps and winning important victories all along the peninsula. Though Rome was left without defense, a campaign in Africa conducted by the Roman general **Scipio "Africanus"** forced Hannibal's armies to halt their advance on Rome, withdraw and return to Carthage, where they were ultimately defeated in 202 BC.

With an enlarged territory and sphere of influence, Rome found itself in competition with ever more dangerous adversaries. The rich and advanced east, the cradle of the classical world, became a new theater of battle: In 200 BC, Rome went to war with Phillip of Macedon and in 191 BC with Antiochus of Syria. Greece was made part of Rome in 146 BC. In the same year the Senate ordered the legions to destroy the Carthaginians once and for all.

A fierce war broke out in 90 BC on the Italian peninsula between Romans and the other Italic peoples, who had been attempting for years to get the rights enjoyed by Roman citizens. Before the Roman legions won the war in 88 BC, the Senate gave in and agreed to extend the rights of citizenship. In the meantime, the insurrection of the Asian provinces and the war against Mithridate, king of Ponto, brought about the rise of the autocrat **Sulla**.

His victory in Asia allowed him, once he returned to Italy, to violently oppose the power of the democrats led by **Marius and Cin-**

na, against whom he started a bloody civil war. After victory in 82 BC, Sulla had the Senate nominate him as dictator-for-life to restore the oligarchy of the Republic.

In 71 BC, **Pompey** and **Crassus** were elected as consuls and diminished the role of the Senate in favor of the tribunes and the knights. It was this conflict between the popular party (represented by Pompey and Crassus) and the Senate which prompted an accord between the two consuls and **Caius Julius Caesar**, a young aristocrat. The election of Caesar as Consul in 59 BC solidified this alliance - the first Triumvirate. Caesar continued the policies of his allies and began a campaign in Gaul which ended in victory in 51 BC, after his consular mandate had ended. Pompey and Crassus had in the meantime again been elected as Consuls, but with Crassus' death in Syria and Pompey's gradual shift toward conservatives in the Senate, a break emerged between the two ex-triumvirs.

This intensified when Julius Caesar was formally invited by the Senate and by Pompey

Model of the Roman Forum.

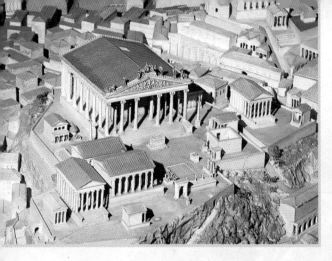

Model of the Temple of Jove on the Capitoline.

to disband his legions. Caesar's refusal to do so began a terrible civil war that forced the escape of Pompey and many senators to the Balkans, where they were defeated at the **battle of Farsalo** in Thessaly (48 BC).

Returning to Rome without rivals, Caesar was nominated Consul in 48 BC and dictator-for-life four years later. But the sum of power acquired by this single man aroused the resentment and political hostility of his former allies. In March of 44 BC, a plot hatched in the Senate and led by **Brutus** and **Cassius** put an end to the life and ambitions of Julius Caesar.

The attempts to restore the Republic in 43 BC were blocked by an alliance between **Marc Antony**, **Lepidus** and **Octavian** (great nephew and adopted son of Caesar, thus nominated Consul by the Senate). The second triumvirate attempted to write a new constitution, and decisively defeated the Republicans Brutus and Cassius at the battle of Filippi in 42 BC. But the cohesion of the triumvirate soon weakened in the absence of a common enemy. The antagonism between Octavian and Antony crushed Lepidus, who soon withdrew, and Octavian secured victory in 31 BC at the **battle of Actium**.

The crisis of the Republic, which had started in the time of the Grac-

Bust of the Emperor Trajan.

chi, ended with the "**golden age**" of **Octavian Augustus**. Octavian initiated a long period of peace and political stability, creating the foundation for a new order upon which **imperial Rome** was to be built. The Senate was retained in deference to the traditions of the Roman aristocracy; the essential novelty was the figure of the prince, who at the vortex of the state oversaw and coordinated the institutions.

After eight uninterrupted years as consul and numerous symbolic tributes, in 27 BC Octavian Augustus had himself assigned the title of **Emperor**, with which he assumed an unlimited pow-

Model of the Tiberina Island.

er over the armies and the provinces. In 12 BC he was honored with the title of Pontifex Maximus (Highest Priest). **Virgil**, **Horace**, **Ovid** and **Livy** were the most meaningful poetic and literary exponents of the Augustean age, which can be considered among the most exciting periods in Roman history. On the artistic and urban level, it was the era in which the Empire learned to celebrate itself. The triumphal arches, the grandiose monuments, and the ever more marvelous Imperial Fora exalted the greatness of Rome and its emperors.

At the death of Augustus in 14 AD, the fundamental lines had been drawn and the imperial regime went on for two strong and vital centuries. The differences between Italy and the provinces were reduced and Roman citizenship was progressively extended as the aristocracy and the "bourgeoisie" of the provinces were integrated into the ruling class of the Empire.

The legacy of Octavian was passed to his adopted son **Tiberius** who continued the **Julian dynasty**. **Caligula** followed from 37 AD to 41 AD; **Claudius** from 41 AD to 54 AD, who was succeeded by the young **Nero**, whose reign was marked by a policy of terror which was so unpopular that he was deposed by the Senate in 68 AD and declared an outlaw.

Between 68 AD and 69 AD the armies in the provinces elected three emperors (**Galba**, **Otho** and **Vitellius**), who killed one another. In 69 AD **Flavius Vespasian**, who had suppressed the revolts in Palestine, began the **Flavian dynasty**, which restored order and reinforced the boundaries of the Empire. He was succeeded by his two sons, **Titus** in 79 AD and immediately after by **Domitian** in 81 AD, who surrounded himself with an imposing military force and ruled so tyrannically that he was killed in a palace plot in 96 AD.

The Emperor Nero.

The Senate then managed to bring the power of the Empire to one of its own, **Nerva**. This began the period during which the emperor, together with the Senate, selected the imperial successor based on considerations of political order and morale, rather than dynasty or bloodlines. This was one of the happiest times in the history of Rome, with long periods of peace and great military successes in the east, Eastern

Model of the interior of the Colosseum.

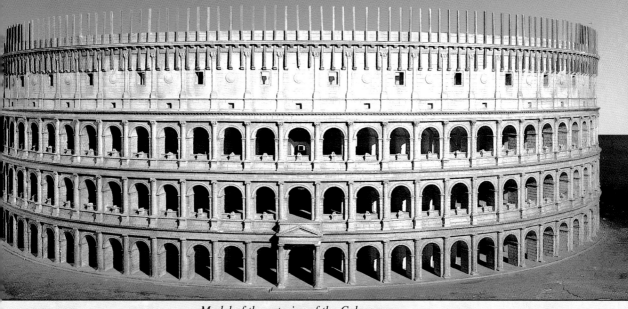

Model of the exterior of the Colosseum.

Europe, and in the north, which marked the pax romana in the known world. During the first and second centuries, after the disastrous fire that engulfed Rome during the reign of Nero, there was urban development on a grand scale. Under the Flavian emperors, the Colosseum, the Baths of Titus, the Palace of Domitian and the Stadium of Domitian (now Piazza Navona) were built.

Just before his death in 98 AD, Nerva chose the Spanish-born **Trajan**, an able general and much

Gladiatorial combat in the arena of the Colosseum.

admired leader, as his successor. In his nineteen year reign, Trajan devoted his energy principally to military campaigns, conquering Dacia (modern-day Romania), Mesopotamia and Arabia, thereby bringing the Empire to its largest extent ever. Such a policy was not followed by the eclectic **Hadrian**, adopted by Trajan and emperor from 117 AD to 138 AD, who pursued a peaceful policy of maintaining the borders, and dedicated himself to the arts, Hellenistic culture and long travels in the provinces. **Antonius Pius** (138 AD - 161 AD) and **Marcus Aurelius** (161 AD - 180 AD) succeeded Hadrian. The latter, who was born in Africa, put an end to succession by adoption when he selected his son **Commodus** (180 AD - 192 AD), who had participated in the government since 176 AD, as his successor.

The successor **Septimius Severus**, a brave military commander, centralized the military administration and concerned himself with defending the borders of the Empire from the ever more present barbarian threat. In 211 AD, he

The area between the Pantheon and the Stadium of Domitian in the era of Constantine (4th Century AD). ⇨

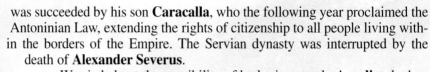

was succeeded by his son **Caracalla**, who the following year proclaimed the Antoninian Law, extending the rights of citizenship to all people living within the borders of the Empire. The Servian dynasty was interrupted by the death of **Alexander Severus**.

Worried about the possibility of barbarian attack, **Aurelian** had an imposing wall built (270 AD - 275 AD) around the city, much of which is still visible. At the end of the 3rd century, **Diocletian** (280 AD - 305 AD) tried to re-establish centralized power and institutionalized the imperial theocracy by which a religious significance was attributed to the emperor. By then there were many Christians and this aggravated their opposition to the Empire and its repressive nature. The battles that followed the abdication of Diocletian were brought to an end only with the victory of **Con-**

Polychrome marble bust of the Emperor Caracalla.

stantine over his rival **Maxentius** in 312 AD. One year later, with the Edict of Milan, the new emperor recognized Christianity, which then became the dominant religion of the Empire. The most important act of the final years of Constantine's reign, which ended with his death in 337 AD, was the transfer of the imperial capital to Byzantium, on the Straits of the Dardanelles. Enlarged and embellished with splendid monuments, the city took the name Constantinople in 330 AD. This epochal shift caused by geopolitical events led to a rapid transformation of the very essence of the Roman Empire.

Capitoline Museums. Marble statue of the Dying Gaul.

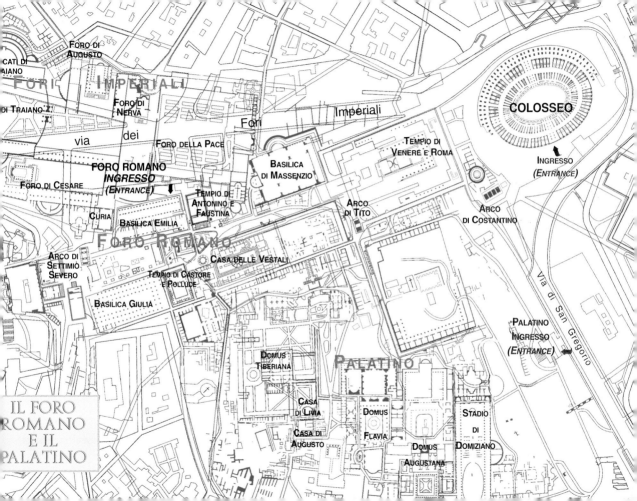

CATI DI
AIANO

FORO DI
AUGUSTO

FORI   IMPERIALI

DI TRAIANO

FORO DI
NERVA

Fori   Imperiali

COLOSSEO

via   dei

FORO DELLA PACE

TEMPIO DI
VENERE E ROMA

INGRESSO
(ENTRANCE)

FORO ROMANO
INGRESSO
(ENTRANCE)

BASILICA
DI MASSENZIO

FORO DI CESARE

TEMPIO DI
ANTONINO E
FAUSTINA

ARCO
DI TITO

ARCO
DI COSTANTINO

CURIA

BASILICA EMILIA

FORO ROMANO

ARCO DI
SETTIMIO
SEVERO

CASA DELLE VESTALI

TEMPIO DI CASTORE
E POLLUCE

BASILICA GIULIA

Via di San Gregorio

PALATINO
INGRESSO
(ENTRANCE)

DOMUS
TIBERIANA

PALATINO

IL FORO
ROMANO
E IL
PALATINO

CASA
DI LIVIA

DOMUS
FLAVIA

STADIO
DI
DOMIZIANO

CASA DI
AUGUSTO

DOMUS
AUGUSTANA

THE COLOSSEUM

This immense amphitheatre, whose imposing remains still allow us to admire its ancient splendour, was begun by Vespasian in 72 A.D. and completed by his son Titus in 80 A.D. It was built by Jewish prisoners. It's true name is the "Flavian amphitheatre", though it was commonly called the Colosseum, both for its proportions and its vicinity to the Colossus of Nero. There is hardly a page of Roman history that is not in some way connected to the Colosseum, which became the symbol of the city and its life.

The Colosseum had the same function as a modern giant stadium, but the favourite spectacles in Roman times were the games of the Circus (*ludi circenses*), which probably had been invented in the late Republican era, with the intention of cultivating the war-like spirit that had made Romans the conquerors of the world. This was the origin of the professional gladiators, who were trained to fight to the death, while wild beasts of every sort increased the horror of the show. Dion Cassius said that 9000 wild animals were killed in the one hundred days of celebrations which inaugurated the amphitheatre. After the animals were killed and removed, the arena was often filled with water in order to stage naval battles.

The Emperor Constantine and his successors tried to put an end to the gladiatorial fights, but at first the Romans did not want to give up their customary shows. At the beginning of the 5th century, a monk called Telemachus came from the east and one day entered the arena and tried to put himself between the gladiators. He appealed to the people to give up their horrid

A view from above of the Colosseo with the enormous veil, which covered it in case of rain.

games. The crowd hurled insults, sarcasm, and ultimately rocks, stoning the intruder to martyrdom. But that day the games were brought to an end.

The Colosseum is elliptical in shape, 187 meters at its longest end and 155 meters at its shortest. The height of the external ring reaches 50 meters from ground level. It was designed to accommodate an estimated 80,000 spectators. Around the exterior run three orders of arches, respectively adorned with Doric, Ionian and Corinthian columns, and a fourth floor with Corinthian pilasters. Of the 80 arches that make up the elliptical ring, four correspond to the entrances at the four axes, of which only the entrance of honour reserved for the Emperor remains.

In the center of the podium, called the *suggestum*, was the Emperor's seat; the rest of the podium was occupied by senators and members of the court. Then came the sections for the cavaliers and civil and military tribunes. There were special places for married coupled, for young men accompanied by their tutors, for families and servants, for women, and for servants.

The Colosseum was usually uncovered, but in case of rain it was covered by an immense velarium, which was maneuvered by two squads of sailors belonging to the fleets of Ravenna and Cape Misenum. These two squads also took part in the naval battles which were often staged in the amphitheatre.

When this amphitheatre was in its full glory, it must have been a stupendous site of Roman greatness. But even today, after so many centuries, the Colosseum is the pride of Rome and a marvel to its visitors. Nonetheless the history of the amphitheatre is not without long periods of abandon and neglect. The end of the Roman Empire was marked by two earthquakes (in 442

and 508), which caused great damage to the structure. The Colosseum was nonetheless still in use under Theodoric, ruler of the Romano-Barbaric kingdom of the Goths, who in 523 authorized the staging of the *venationes*, the traditional hunt of the wild beasts. From that point began the total abandon that saw the Colosseum used as a cemetery, a fortress, and above all, after the earthquake of 1349, as a quarry for building materials. The marble which once covered it almost entirely was reused in the busy period of construction during the Renaissance.

In order to halt the serious decay of the Colosseum, Pope Benedict XIV (1740-1758) consecrated the old amphitheatre by setting up a **Way of the Cross** and raising a cross on the site, which has been connected to thousands of Christian martyrs.

Gladiator fighting a lion.

The inside of the Colosseum. ⮌

THE DOMUS AUREA REDISCOVERED

The *Domus Aurea* (Golden House) is the splendid residence that Nero feverishly built in the few years between the great fire of 64 AD and his tragic death in 69 AD.

The Golden House was actually a spectacular complex of pavilions sparkling with gold, ivory, precious stone and polychromatic marble, immersed in a green countryside artificially constructed inside the city.

The perimeter of the fairy-like park extended from the Velia to the Oppian Hill, including all of the area where the Colosseum stands. Of the many marvels, however, almost all disappeared right after the death of Nero: successive emperors did all they could to erase even the memory of this undertaking.

Even the central pavilion, which served as the actual imperial residence, was completely covered by the baths built on the site by Trajan; in 104 AD, after a terrible fire, he had the ruins of the upper floor leveled and filled in a good portion of the floor below, thus creating a solid base for the new building.

For many centuries the Domus Aurea seemed lost; only in 1500 was its existence rediscovered as artists of the Renaissance lowered themselves with rope into the dark and gloomy grottoes to see the delicate pictorial decorations, which were from then on called "grotesques".

Domus Aurea. The octagonal Hall. ⇨

The Arch of Titus.

THE ROMAN FORUM

The center of the civic and economic life in Republican times, the Forum maintained an important role also in the Imperial period.

The Forum was crossed by the **Via Sacra**, which led to the Capitol Hill and also served as the route of the triumphal processions of victorious generals laden with booty and followed by ranks of prisoners.

While the oldest section of the Forum (built in the Republican era) stretched from the opposite side of the valley to the edge of the Capitol Hill, the entrance on the square of the Colosseum leads to the most recently built section, which dates from the Imperial Age.

On the Via Sacra, at the top of the Velia, is the **Arch of Titus**, which the Senate built after the Emperor's death in memory of his conquest of Jerusalem (70 A.D.). On the inside of the arch are two fine bas-reliefs: the Emperor on his triumphal chariot and the procession of the Jewish prisoners carrying a seven-branched candelabrum.

The Roman Forum, center of the city's public life in ancient times. ⇨

THE BASILICA OF MAXENTIUS

The immense **Basilica of Maxentius** (also called the Basilica of Constantine) was the last edifice built in the city which conveys the magnificence of Ancient Rome. It was begun by Maxentius and completed by his successor Constantine. Part of this imposing 4th century structure has been restored, revealing the portion which faced the Forum and the smaller northern aisle.

The great apse and powerful barrel vaults were a source of inspiration to Renaissance architects; it is thought that this ruin inspired Bramante's plans for the new St. Peter's.

Model of the Basilica of Maxentius.

The interior of the Basilica of Maxentius. ⇨

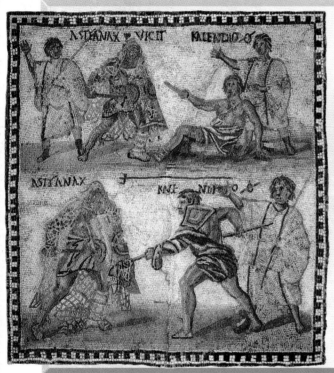

THE TEMPLE OF ANTONINUS AND FAUSTINA

The **Temple of Antoninus and Faustina** is the best preserved building in the Forum. The loss of Faustina embittered her husband, the Emperor Antonius Pius.

After her death, the Emperor wanted to deify her and built a magnificent temple in her honour (141 A.D.). This temple was transformed in the middle ages into the church of *"San Lorenzo in Miranda"*.

A Roman mosaic with fighting gladiators.

THE HOUSE OF THE VESTAL VIRGINS

The round **Temple of Vesta** dates from the time of King Numa Pompilius (8th century B.C.), when it was built to guard the Palladium (the image of Minerva) and other sacred objects brought to Italy by Aeneas, and upon which it was believed the security of the city depended. The six Vestals were chosen from patrician maidens, the daughters of free men, and had to keep the fire burning. They enjoyed special privileges, but if one broke her vow of chastity, she was buried alive in the Campo Scellerato (Field of Villains).

They lived nearby in the **House of the Vestal Virgins**, which was almost totally recon-structed, along with the Temple of Vesta, by the Emperor Septimius Severus after a fire in 191 A.D. Many statues and interesting inscriptions remain. The house, comparable to a modern convent, was divided into different chambers which opened onto the large central atrium.

Both the temple and the house of the Vestals once belonged to the first **Regia** of Rome, which according to tradition was the royal residence founded by the second king of Rome, Numa Pompilius, and later home to the "Pontifex Maximus" (highest priest).

From the plan of the sacred building it is possible to recognise a trapezoidal part at the north end and a rectangle to the south, divided in three rooms.

THE TEMPLE OF JULIUS CAESAR AND THE TEMPLE OF CASTOR AND POLLUX

The **Temple of Julius Caesar**, which Octavian built in memory of his uncle, was begun in 42 B.C. on the spot where the dictator's body was burned, and consecrated in 29 A.D. together with the nearby **Arch of Augustus**, of which only the foundation remains.

The **Temple of Castor and Pollux** (also called the "Temple of the Dioscuri") was built in 484 B.C. to commemorate the victory of Aulus Postumius over the Latins in the battle of Lake Regillus.

The three Corinthian columns and part of the cornice date to the era of Tiberius or Hadrian (1st or 2nd century A.D.).

The three columns of the Temple of Castor and Pollux.

The Temple of Julius Caesar and, to the right, the Temple of Castor and Pollux. ⇨

THE BASILICA JULIA

The **Basilica Julia**, built by Julius Caesar in the middle of the 1st century B.C., was an enormous structure with five naves , divided in sections with movable partitions, which allowed more than one audience to take place at the same time.

Chess squares and other games traced into the marble on the steps of the building offer an interesting look at life in the Forum and the way in which Romans passed the time. After all the vicissitudes of the Forum, the vast basilica underwent a final restoration in 277 A.D.

The **Comitium**, where the representatives of the people gathered for public discussions, had previously been the tribunal. The Comitium consisted of three elements: the *square*, where the popular assembly met, the *Curia*, where the Senate deliberated, and the *rostrum* from which the orators spoke.

The **Basilica Emilia** was built by Emilio Lepidus and Fulvius Nobilius in 179 B.C., and subsequently rebuilt and restored many times under the care of the Aemelia family, until a fire at the beginning of the 5th century did irreparable damage. It was one of the greatest buildings in the Forum, used as many others of its kind for the administration and courts of the city. In front of the Basilica is a small round foundation of the shrine of the "Venus Cloacina" on the point where the Cloaca Maxima entered the Forum.

The area between the Basilica Emilia (to the left) and the Basilica Julia (to the right). ⇨

THE TEMPLE OF SATURN AND THE TEMPLE OF VESPASIAN

The **Temple of Saturn** was erected by the Consul Titus Larcius on the 17th of December, B.C. It was always used as the public treasury, and as a repository for the standards of the Legions and the decrees of the Senate. Sacred treasures were held in an underground chamber. The temple was enlarged in 42 B.C., and rebuilt after an fire in the 4th century A.D. Three columns remain of the **Temple of Vespasian** which was built by the son of Domitian in 94 A.D. and later restored by Septimius Severus.

Arch of Septimius Severus.

The **Temple of Concord** was built by Furio Camillo, the conqueror of the Gauls in 367 B.C. in memory of the agreement concluded at Monte Sacro between the plebians and patricians.

The complex **Arch of Septimius Severus** had been erected in honour of Septimius and his sons, Caracalla and Geta. In the inscription recalls an Imperial tragedy: the murder of Geta by Caracalla, who later had his brother's name removed from the monument. Septimius Severus reigned for 18 years (193-211) and, quite unusually for the 3rd century, died of natural causes.

The Temple of Saturno (in front) and the Temples of Vespasian and Concord (to the side). ☞

THE PALATINE

An historic Roman hill, the **Palatine**, faces the Forum, preserving unforgettable memories in its luxuriant vegetation. The Palatine was the center of Rome in two distinct periods: that of the Roman Kings and of the Empire. During the republic the Palatine was home to patrician families: Quintus Hortensius, the celebrated orator who emulated Cicero, had a house here which later was acquired and enlarged by Augustus. As soon as Augustus became Emperor, he made his Imperial residence on the Palatine. Subsequently, Tiberius, Caligula, the Flavii and finally Septimius Severus built palaces here.

The Palatine was the cradle of Rome. According to legend, it was on the Palatine that Romulus first traced the square outline of the city, and from then on served as the seat of the Roman Kings. Accordingly, the Palatine was the chosen residence of emperors from Caesar to Septimius Severus. The only exception being Nero; and though he built his great *Domus Aurea* (Golden House) elsewhere, he never inhabited it.

The **Clivus Palatinus** leads up to the Palatine, and the stairs on the right to the splendid **Villa Farnese**, with its 16th century Casina and Farnese Gardens, supported by the powerful arches of the **Domus Tiberiana**. From the terrace on the left, the steps lead down to the Palatine Area, where, among other venerable memories, there are ruins of the temple of **Magnus Mater** with the statue of a seated Cibele, found in the 3rd century B.C. and completely rebuilt after a great fire destroyed it in 111 B.C.

Imperial palaces of the Palatine as seen from Circus Maximus. ↷

On the eastern boundary of the area are ruins of the wall of "Roma Quadrata," some blocks of tufa thought to have belonged to the hut of Romulus and traces of the **Scalae Caci**, an early access to the Palatine. An early cistern (6th - 5th century B.C.) is located on the square.

The nearby **House of Livia** is a typical example of a patrician house of the late Republican period which together with the **House of Augustus** and the **Temple of Apollo** formed the Augustean complex, the first Imperial complex on the on the Palatine. The murals, in the Pompeian style, are interesting despite their poor condition. To the right is the **Palace of the Flavii**, designed by Rabirius for the Emperor Domitian. It included a *basilica*, *aula regia* and *lararium* on the left; a peristyle in the center; and a *triclinium* on the right, which features remains of pavement and two *nymphaea*, one of which is in very good condition. Under the pavement there are traces of pre-existing structures. Attached to the palace was the **Domus Augustana**, where the Imperial court lived.

The **Circus of Domitian** (160 meters x 48 meters) is surrounded by fragments of porticoes, statues, fountains, and on one side, the large niche of the Imperial loggia.

Nearby are the ruins of the **Palace** and the massive **Baths of Septimius Severus**, at the foot of which rose the Septizonium, an imposing building whose remains were demolished by Pope Sixtus V.

From above these colossal ruins, the **Belvedere** offers a magnificent panorama.

The Circus of Domitian on the Palatine Hill. ⇨

THE CIRCUS MAXIMUS

The enormous elliptical **Circus Maximus** (664 meters x 123 meters) runs along the base of the Palatiine Hill, almost entirely filling the space between the Palatine and Aventine Hills. The huge basin is still buried. Recent attempts to landscape the barren slopes have not been maintained.

The structure was built in the time of the Etruscan kings, who transformed Rome from a village into a monumental city, on the place where religious rites and games in honour of the God Consus (the *Consualia*) were held since the times of Romulus. It was during this very celebration that the Rape of the Sabines occurred, to which the Romans resorted, according to the famous legend, in order to increase the population of the city.

In the time of Augustus, the Circus Maximus held 150,000 spectators, and with additions by Trajan, 250,000. The Circus was used for the Roman chariot races, which were among the greatest spectacles for the Roman people.

To the left, the Circus Maximus today;
to the right, how it appeared in ancient Roman times.

THE IMPERIAL FORA
FORUM OF JULIUS CAESAR

The **Forum of Julius Caesar**, consecrated in 46 B.C. and later finished by Augustus, was the first of the Imperial Fora built with the spoils of victory from the Gallic Wars. Formed by a rectangular piazza surrounded on all sides by porticoes, it had at its center the **Temple of Venus Genetrix**. The Julian family, to which Julius belonged, claimed to originate from Julo, or Ascanius, son of the Trojan hero Aeneas, who according to Homeric mythology was son of the mortal Anchises and the Goddess Venus. The temple featured many works of art, among them the sculpture of Venus Genetrix by Arcesilao. In its simplicity the Forum of Julius Caesar surpasses the narrow dimensions of the Republican age, and from an historical point of view, underlines the passage to the imperial age by anticipating the monumental complexes built by Caesar's successors. The Forum was expanded by Trajan, who added the Basilica Argentaria and rededicated the temple, along with Trajan's Column, in May of 113 A.D.

Model of the Forums of Augustus and Nerva.

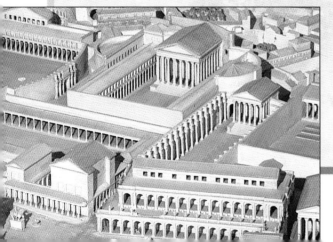

The Forum of Julius Caesar. ✧

THE FORUM OF AUGUSTUS

After the assassination of Caesar, the conspirators Brutus and Cassius went to take possession of the provinces of Syria and Macedonia. In 42 B.C., they led their armies at Philippi against the heirs of Caesar, Octavian and Marc Antony. Just as Julius Caesar took a vow at Farsalo, so Augustus took one at Philippi: in the event of victory, he was to build a temple in a new Forum and dedicate it to Mars, father of the Roman people and God of war. After the victory and the death of the two conspirators, Augustus maintained his vow and built the **Temple of Mars Ultor** (the Avenger) in the center of the new Forum, and inaugurated it on the first of August in the year 2 B.C.

Excavations have brought to light magnificent remains of this forum and the gigantic temple, among them three Corinthian columns that once stood 15 meters in height. Augustus was the first Emperor (30 B.C. - 14 A.D.); under his reign, Jesus Christ was born.

Emperor Octavian Augustus.

The Temple of Mars Ultor in the Forum of Augustus. ⇨

TRAJAN'S FORUM AND TRAJAN'S MARKETS

The formidable task of reign of the Emperor M. Ulpius Trajan was the expansion of the Empire towards the east, beyond Dacia. Trajan departed for the Danube. Once his roads and fortifications were ready, he took the Dacian capital by force and imposed extremely hard conditions. In 105 A.D. there was a new battle. The Dacians fought desperately, but their army was destroyed. After the celebration of the triumph, Trajan decided to commemorate his victory by building a Forum that would surpass all other fora in splendour and scale. He entrusted the project to the great architect, Apollodorus of Damascus. By cutting away a good portion of the base of the Quirinal hill, an area twice the size of the existing fora was created; 61 million cubic meters of earth and rock was moved to make way for the Trajan's Forum.

But the great monument to the victory over the Dacians is the noble **Column**, which after 19 centuries was returned to its original majesty and antique splendour by careful restoration. The ashes of the emperor were once set into the base of the column and his statue once stood on top. The column consists of 19 blocks of marble and a spiral staircase which leads to the top. The most important part of this historic monument is the helicoidal band of figures that spiral around it, which document the arms, art and costumes of the Romans and Dacians.

Set into the Quirinal Hill is the complex known as TRAJAN'S MARKETS, which consists of a well-preserved, semi-circular, three story structure, and above, a large vaulted hall, which resembles a basilica.

Trajan's Markets. ➪

THE THEATRE OF MARCELLUS

On the left, near the beginning of Via del Teatro Marcello, a rock rises which is thought to be the famous **Rupe Tarpea** (Tarpean Rock), from which the traitor Tarpea was thrown, and subsequently all others punished for betraying Rome.

The fine **Theatre of Marcellus** (recently restored) is the only ancient theater left in Rome. It was conceived by Julius Caesar and later built by Augustus in honour of Marcellus, son of his sister Octavia, who died in 23 B.C. at age 20, and was immortalised in the poetry of Virgil.

The original structure accommodated between 15,000 and 20,000 spectators. What remains of the structure, which must have served as a model for the Colosseum, is a part of the curved exterior wall with an elegant double row of Doric and Ionic arches. Above is the 16th century Savelli palace (later of the Orsini) built into the theater by Baldassare Peruzzi.

To the right of Theater of Marcellus rise three columns from the *Temple of Apollo Sosiano* (5th century B.C.). Nearby are the remains of the **Portico di Ottavia** - built by Augustus to honour his sister. The propylaeum serves as the atrium of the 8th century church of **Sant'Angelo in Pescheria**, named for the fish market which was once located on the same site.

The façade of the Theatre of Marcellus. ⇨

THE ISLAND ON THE TIBER

A footbridge crosses from the Lungotevere to the **Isola Tiberina** (the island on the Tiber), where the church of **St. Bartholomew** stands on the ruins of the celebrated Temple of Aesculapius, the Greek God of medicine, once a pilgrimage site for the diseased.

Two bridges join the island to the rest of the city: **Ponte Fabricius** (also known as Quattro Capi), built in 62 B.C. and still intact today, and **Ponte Cestio** (46 B.C.). The nearby *Ponte Palatino Bridge* was formerly the site of the **Ponte Sublicio**, noted for the legend of Horace Cocles, the Roman hero who single-handedly fought the Etruscans under Porsenna.

The 1st century B.C. temple named for **Fortuna Virile** is identified with the *Temple of Portunus*, the protector of the nearby port, and offers an excellent example of the Greco-Italic architecture of the Republican era. In 872 A.D., a certain Stefano converted it into a Christian church dedicated to Santa Maria Egiziaca.

The beautiful 2nd century B.C. **Round Temple**, the oldest Roman temple built of marble that exists today. In the past it was identified as a temple to Vesta, probably due to its resemblance to the temple of the same name in the Roman Forum. The latest archaeological evidence attributes it to Hercules Victor.

THE PANTHEON

As the beautiful inscription across the facade suggests, the Pantheon was built by the famous Agrippa, one of Emperor Augustus' principal collaborators. Almost completely destroyed by a fire, it was remade by Hadrian in 118 AD. The building is substantially intact, thanks to the Byzantine Emperor Phocas, who gave the pagan temple to Pope Boniface IV in 608, who then transformed it into a Christian church.

The *façade* has the classical appearance of a Roman temple, with a colonnaded portico surmounted by a triangular front, which over the course of the centuries was used for various contrasting purposes. The traditional pronaos leads to the *interior*, whose round plan makes up the supporting drum for the celebrated cupola. It is actually a cap, whose thickness diminishes as it rises; in the center is an open oculus (8.92 meters in diameter), which features some of the original bronze trim.

The interior is therefore a single majestic space entirely centred on a curved line, highlighted by the clear light which falls from the central oculus, also typical of Roman architecture. Naturally, the statues of the gods which once stood in the large niches have long since been substituted by the *central altar* and the *funeral monuments*, among them that of Raphael. The Pantheon also hosts several tombs of the royal family.

THE HADRIAN'S MAUSOLEUM - CASTEL SANT'ANGELO

Castel Sant'Angelo appears to be an impenetrable, fortified bastion, but originally it was built to hold the mortal remains of the Emperor Hadrian. The *Hadrianeum* or Hadrian's Mausoleum was begun by Hadrian himself in 130 AD and finished in 139 AD, a year after his death.

The original structure of the mausoleum is still the central fulcrum of the castle. The castle-fortress was characterised by its strategic role during the entire middle ages.

Inside, several parts belong to the original mausoleum: the ample *vaulted vestibule*; the *heliocoidal ramp*, along which the tiny, inhospitable *celle* (cells) which held prisoners can be seen; the huge *central room*, destined to contain the funerary urn of the Emperor Hadrian and his descendants. This last part is crossed by the Renaissance *Cordonata di Alessandro VI* which cuts across the entire structure.

The levels of the courtyards are primarily Renaissance in character. The *Cortile d'Onore* or *dell'Angelo (*Courtyard of honour, or of the Angel*)* is dominated by the facade of the *Chapel of Pope Leo X*, designed by Michelangelo.

A walkway encircling the castle begins from the airy *Loggia di Giulio II*, which offers one of the most celebrated (with good reason) panoramas of Rome. A few steps away are the *Papal Apartments*, built around the mid-16th century for Pope Paul III, with a succession of richly decorated and furnished rooms.

The Hadrian's Mausoleum, today as Castel Sant'Angelo. ✧

THERMES OF CARACALLA

The famous **Baths of Caracalla**, or "Antoniane", were begun by Septimius Severus in 206 and opened in 217 by Caracalla, and were completed by their successors Heliogabalus and Alexander Severus. Lined with basalt, granite and alabaster, the enormous baths of hot, warm and cold water could accommodate 1,600 at a time. Splendid vaults, porticoes, esedrae and gymnasiums were decorated with the most precious marble, the most beautiful sculptures and the largest columns imaginable. The ruins of this great complex are still impressive for their size and majesty.

The interior of the Baths of Caracalla.

Not so far we find the **Via Appia Antica** (the Appian Way); there is no road with more interesting archaeological, artistic and pastoral elements than this road . Proudly called the "regina viarum" (queen of all roads), it was begun by Appius Claudius in 312 B.C.. Tombs lined the sides of the road for miles, but only members of patrician families, such as the Scipios, Furii, Manili and Sestili were buried here.

Model of the Baths of Caracalla. ✧

VILLA ADRIANA

When Publius Aelius Hadrian assumed power on the 2nd of August 117 AD, the Roman empire was at its maximum extent and power. Hadrian was a highly-cultured man. This extraordinary complex was constructed between the years 118 and 134 A.D.

It is difficult to imagine the scope of the original Villa, which must have been a city unto itself; only one fifth of the original three-hundred hectare complex is visible today.

Villa Adriana's best-known features bear numerous references to the places that had most impressed the emperor's memory and spirit during his travels.

Today, Hadrian's capricious taste for reproducing the bizarre copies of the monuments he saw abroad, is perceived as a reflection of his political program, which for the first time put the provinces on par with Rome.

Hadrian's immediate successors, the Antonini, used the Villa as their summer residence, but after them the Villa fell into disrepair.

Diocletian restored it at the end of the 3rd century A.D. But shortly afterwards, according to several sources, Constantine embellished the new capital of the eastern empire, Constantinople, with artwork taken from Hadrian's Villa.

Hadrian's Villa - The Maritime Theater. ⇨

POMPEII

On August 24th, 79 AD, Mount Vesuvius suddenly erupted. A tempest of ash, lapillus, poisonous gas, and magma fell on the areas surrounding the volcano, while streams of lava and incandescent mud continuously ran down its slopes. The catastrophe was so sudden and unexpected, that the over thirty-thousand people living in the city below were taken by surprise.

When the eruption stopped, Pompeii was buried under more than six meters of volcanic debris. The same ashes that destroyed the city also preserved evidence of daily life at that tragic moment. Pompeii was excavated at the end of the 18th century, and the city miraculously came to life again.

The Forum, made up of a large rectangular piazza, was the center of the city's civic, religious and economic life. The north side is closed by the 2nd-century BC Temple of Jupiter, flanked by two honourary arches. The largest sacred building built in the city since the Samnite era, the Temple is a conspicuous example of Italic style, set on a podium with a double set of steps. It features a pronaos, encircled by Corinthian columns and a large cella with an internal colonnade. The other three sides were encircled by a portico, built in the Samnite era, and partially restored in the Roman period. Several tracts of the portico were surmounted by a loggiato, with slender columns which ran above the entablature.

A series of bases on the south side marks the places of numerous honourary statues, while the largest pediment has been identified with the suggestum, the tribune of the orators.

Pompeii, view of the Forum. ⇨

Pompeii - The colonnade of the Forum.

The House of the Faun is perhaps the most beautiful private dwelling that remains from the ancient world.

The wall decorations of the vestibule feature two *lararii* in the form of a small temple, in extremely fine stucco; the floor is laid out in *opus sectile* with polychrome marble tiles. The impluvium leads to the two atriums at the center of the house. The principle *atrium* is connected to the traditional *tablinum*; next is the first peristyle, with twenty-eight Ionic style columns and a fountain at the center. In the background is an exedra with a floor that was originally made up of a splendid mosaic representing the Battle between Alexander and Darius, which gave the space a character of exceptional nobility and splendour.

The second and larger peristyle follows, with a Doric *portico* surmounted by a *loggiato*, at the end of which opens a back exit.

Pompeii - The atrium of the House of the Faun, with the bronze statue of the Dancing Faun ⬧

CHRISTIAN ROME
THE CATACOMBS

As well as the vestiges of classical Rome, the Appian Way also offers some of the most important evidence about early Christianity. Some of the best-known Roman catacombs, as these ancient Christian subterranean cemeteries have been called since the 9th century, lie beneath the ancient road. The term **Catacomb** (from the Greek *katà cymba* = near the cavity) actually first referred specifically to the site of the **Catacombs of St. Sebastian**, which was a pozzolana quarry whose galleries were used for the first Christian cemetery.

The catacombs were greatly expanded with the spread of Christianity in Rome; cunicula were carved out on various levels for kilometres, resulting in an inextricable spider web in which it is easy to lose your way. For this reason visits to the catacombs are

Catacombs of San Sebastiano.
A ceiling decorated with stuccoes.

ANCOTIAEAVXESI
ANCOTIVSEPAPHROD
ETANCOTIAIRENE
PARENTES
B·M·F

*Catacombs of St. Sebastian.
The three Mausoleums.* ✧

*Catacombs.
Paleo-Christian
inscriptions and frescoes.*

GERONTIVPAS
INDEO

conducted by official guides from the Franciscan order, who are the caretakers of the cemetery complex.

The Catacombs of St. Sebastian, above which a great basilica was built in the 4th century, were discovered during a 17th century restoration by Flaminio Ponzio and Giovanni Vasanzio. On the second level underground is the **Crypt of St. Sebastian**, where the body of the saint remained until it was transferred to the basilica during the restoration work. The *Cubiculum of Jonah*, with interesting frescoes of the biblical story of Jonah, and the scene of Noah saved from the Ark (late 4th century); the *Sarcophagus of Lot*; the "*Piazzola*", an early entrance to the catacombs. The *Three Mausoleums* (in particularly good condition) face the Piazzola.

The **Catacombs of St. Calixtus** were the first official burial place for the Christian community in Rome. All the popes of the 3rd century were buried here in the *Papal Crypt*. The first group of crypts was the *Cubiculum of St. Cecilia* (178 A.D.). The statue of the young martyr is by Maderno.

After the Crypt of the Popes are the *Cubicula of the Sacraments*, the *Chapel of Pope Gaius*, and the *Crypt of St. Eusebius*.

The **Catacombs of Domitilla** are named after the Christian lady to whom this land belonged. She was a member of the Flavians, an Imperial family. There are possibly the most extensive catacombs in Rome. In this area stands the 4th century *Basilica of Sts. Nereus and Achilleus*, which was discovered in 1874 and subsequently restored.

Catacombs of St. Calixtus. The Crypt of Santa Cecilia. To the right, a hallway. ⇨

THE VATICAN CITY

The **Vatican** has been the residence of the popes only since 1377, six centuries interrupted by long stays at the Quirinal Palace. Before the pontifical court was transferred to Avignon (1309-1377), the headquarters of the pope had been at the Lateran.

Since then, there has not been a pope who has failed to contribute to the grandeur and dignity of the Vatican, to make this holy hill an increasingly worthy seat for the Supreme Head of the Catholic Church. An uninterrupted succession of 265 men have sat on St. Peter's throne, many of whom were martyrs and saints. The Vatican has been an independent state (called the **Vatican City**) since February 11, 1929, when the Lateran Treaty definitively resolved the "Roman Issue" between the Church and the Italian State.

To the left, a fresco of the old Constantinian Basilica.

Model of the Circus of Nero, upon which St. Peter's Basilica was built. ⇨

THE VATICAN HILL AND THE ANCIENT CONSTANTINIAN BASILICA

In Roman times, the Vatican Hill was outside the city and for centuries had been considered unhealthy and inhospitable. Agrippina, the grandmother of Emperor Nero, transformed it into a flourishing garden. Nero, who used to go there often, subsequently enriched it. A circus extended on the sides of the Vatican Hill in the area which corresponds to what is now the left side of St. Peter's Square. It was built by the Emperor Caligula, and at its center stood the obelisk which now stands at the center of the square.

In 67 AD, the Apostle Peter was crucified and was then buried in an anonymous grave in the adjacent necropolis, an event which would mark this spot for eternity. After Nero was killed, the *Circus of Caligula* (or *Circus of Nero*) was abandoned, while the *Vatican Necropolis* became a site holy to the Christian cult.

Two hundred fifty years later, the Emperor Constantine, who made Christianity the state religion, had a grandiose basilica built at the foot of the Vatican Hill, in a way so that its apse contained the tomb which the Christians had always considered the tomb of St. Peter. In order to do so, the Emperor had to cut away a part of the Vatican Hill, and with the profanation of the cemetery, created an esplanade that allowed for the excavation of the solid foundation.

The church was built in the style of a Roman pagan basilica, although it included important architectural innovations which were adopted and further developed for other Christian

Drawing of the old St. Peter's Basilica, built by the Emperor Constantine. ✧

St. Peter's dome.

religious sites. The grandiosity of the old St. Peter's Basilica was established through five naves intersected by a transept, an important innovation.

As was customary during the late-Imperial period, construction materials were taken from pre-existing buildings from the adjacent Circus of Nero. The various columns were therefore made of different materials, and the marble pavement had pagan inscriptions and reliefs. The façade was decorated with rich mosaics and was preceded by a large atrium. In the background, at the center of the apse, the tomb of St. Peter serves as the focal point of the basilica, drawing the attention of the faithful.

Whether the tomb contained the actual remains of the Saint was debated for centuries, and remained more an act of faith

St. Peter's Basilica. ⇨

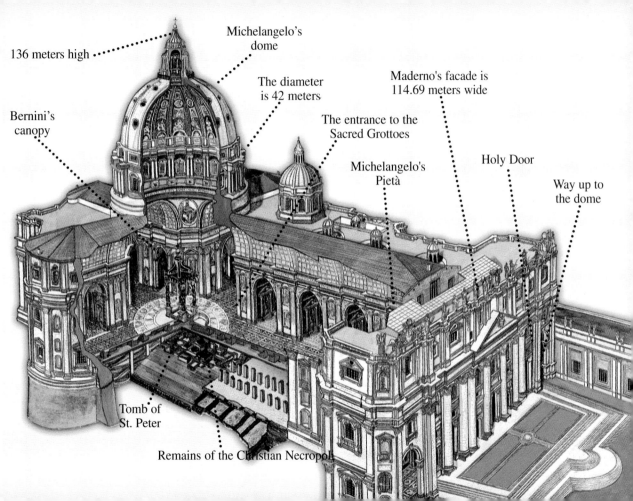

136 meters high

Michelangelo's dome

The diameter is 42 meters

Maderno's facade is 114.69 meters wide

Bernini's canopy

The entrance to the Sacred Grottoes

Michelangelo's Pietà

Holy Door

Way up to the dome

Tomb of St. Peter

Remains of the Christian Necropoli

than certainty. But in 1968, Pope Paul VI announced to the world that *"the reliquaries of St. Peter have been identified in a manner which we can consider convincing."* Such a declaration led to long studies, which subsequently provided significant confirmation.

The archeologists had concentrated their attention on a tomb toward which all the other tombs of the Vatican Necropolis converged, and on two walls in particular. The first, erected around 160 AD in brick and covered with red plaster, has an inscription *"Petr ... en... "*. The second, which dates to the 3rd century AD and built perpendicular to the first. It was covered with grafitti of the names of the faithful who gathered in prayer in the presence of this venerated tomb, as well as invocations of Christ (of the word in grafitti, which was called *"Muro G"*). Across a cavity from this wall, it is possible to reach human remains exhumed and re-interred here during the construction of the Constantinan Basilica.

Philological studies showed that the inscription *"Petr... en..."* meant, in ancient greek, that "Peter is here.", while scientific analysis supported the hypothesis that the bones found here were those of the Apostle Peter. The coincidence of these two important discoveries, along with other elements, allowed for acceptance of the historical announcement of Pope Paul VI.

In the St. Peter's Basilica, the tomb of St. Peter is below the papal altar in the Confession, which is accessed by two semi-circular ramps which descend to the level of the Constantinian Basilica.

THE ST. PETER'S BASILICA

The greatest church in Christendom, **St. Peter's Basilica**, rises on the grandiose **St. Peter's Square**. Michelangelo's mighty silver-blue dome dominates the scene, blending into the sky above, conveying a sense of the absolute and infinite, which touches the soul of all who gaze upon it. The construction of the dome proceeded through problems and obstacles of every kind. Michelangelo was already quite old when he began the project in 1546, and when he died in 1564 only the drum had been completed. The rest of the work was finished between 1588 and 1589 by Giacomo della Porta and Domenico Fontana. The **Colonnade** is Bernini's most beautiful work, and forms the solemn entrance to St. Peter's and the Vatican. The two great open semicircular wings seem as if they were the outstretched arms of the church, receiving all of mankind in one universal embrace. If some of Bernini other works appear to be extravagant, this colonnade shows the height of his genius. He also designed the 140 *statues of saints* in which decorate the colonnade, which were sculpted with the help of his pupils.

Pope Sixtus V (1585-1590) chose Domenico Fontana to

A portrait of St. Peter.

The Colonnade of St. Peter's Basilica. ➪

Michelangelo's Pietà.

oversee the erection of the **Obelisk** in the middle of the piazza, a considerable task which aroused wonder and great enthusiasm in the people. The obelisk measures more than 25 meters in height and was brought from the nearby ruins of the Circus of Nero.

The Borghese Pope Paul V commissioned Maderno (1607-1614) to construct the broad **facade** of the church, and had his name and title written in very large letters across the entablature.

Five doors open onto the **portico**, corresponding to the five aisles in the basilica.

Entering the church, one is struck by the enormity of the basilica. The numbers speak eloquently: the length of the interior of the basilica, as shown in an inscription in the pavement near the bronze door, is 186.36 meters (the external length, including the portico, is

The central nave of St. Peter's Basilica.

211.5 meters). Other signs in the floor indicate the lengths of the major churches in the world; the vault is 44 meters high; the dome, measured from the inside, measures 119 meters, with the lantern adding another 17 meters; the perimeter of one of the four piers which support the dome measures 71 meters.

At the end of the immense central nave rises the bronze baldacchino (canopy) which covers the high altar - its 29 meters makes it 4 meters taller than the obelisk on the piazza. One of the most significant objects that was transferred from the old basilica is the *porphyry disk* at the beginning of the nave, upon which Charlemagne knelt on Christmas Day 800 to be consecrated Holy Roman Emperor by Pope Leo III.

The high altar, under the cupola, rises above the **Tomb of St. Peter**, which was definitively identified after excavations in the 1950's. In front of the tomb, ninety-nine lamps burn day and night; opposite is the **crypt**, designed by Maderno, rich with inlaid marble. Above the altar rises Bernini's fantastic **baldacchino** (1633), supported by four spiral columns, made from bronze taken from the Pantheon. But the glorification of the tomb of the humble fisherman from the Galilee is the majestic **dome** that soars toward the heavens.

In the Tribune, four Doctors of the Church support the **Throne of St. Peter**, a stunning work in gilded bronze by Bernini. Returning toward the entrance, in the first chapel of the right nave is Michelangelo's **Pietà**, sculpted between 1498 and 1499. The artist's name is engraved on the sash that crosses the bust of the Virgin.

ST. PETER'S BASILICA
TROUGH THE CENTURIES

The diagram shows:

✦ *In yellow, the ground plan of Nero's Circus (67 A.D.) on Vatican hill;*

✦ *In blue, the Constantinian Basilica (321 A.D.);*

✦ *In brown, the first part of St. Peter's Basilica built by Bramante and Michelangelo between 1506 and 1564. In the center, the tomb of St. Peter, next to the necropolis;*

✦ *In orange, the extension of the Basilica completed by Carlo Maderno in 1614;*

✦ *In green the Bernini's colonnade completed in 1667.*

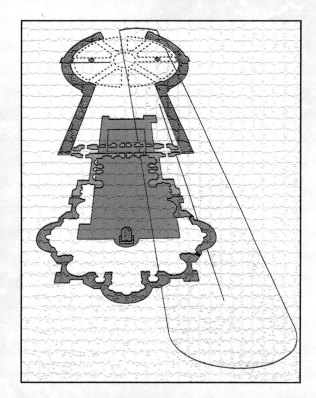

THE SACRED GROTTOES

The lower level of the present basilica, which roughly corresponds to the level of the old basilica which Constantine built, is of particular interest. It is reached from inside the basilica, by a stairway which passes through St. Longino's pillar, and opens onto the semicircular gallery known as the **New Grottoes**. This is actually the oldest part of the grotto, but was so named because it was opened later.

Excavations under the tomb of St. Peter led to the important discovery that Pope Paul VI announced on June 26, 1968: "The relics of Peter have been identified in a way which we may consider convincing."

Four oratories open onto the Gallery and several chapels, in two of which are the **tombs of Pope Pius XII** and **Pope John XXIII**.

At the end of the hall are the **Old Grottoes**,

The Sistine Chapel.   *The Tomb of St. Peter.* ⟿

which extend across the vast space under the central nave of the upper basilica. They were made by Antonio da Sangallo the Younger as an interspace to protect the flooring of the new basilica from humidity.

In the fascinating shadows cast between the three aisles with the low vaulted ceiling and two rows of sturdy pillars are the funeral monuments of about twenty popes - among them Pope John XXIII, Pope Paul VI, Pope John Paul I, an emperor, a king, two queens, numerous cardinals and bishops, as well as precious works of art and relics from the old basilica. The obligatory itinerary passes through just one side nave, from which it is nonetheless possible to appreciate the entire space.

Nighttime on St. Peter's Square.

THE WAY UP TO THE DOME

The first part of the ascent, from ground level to the terrace above the central nave, can be made on foot or by elevator. The view from the balustrade is fantastic: Bernini's colonnade in the foreground, the scintillating Tiber a bit further out, and the rest of the city all create a very harmonious scene.

Passing to the interior, the gallery which runs along the drum of the dome, 53 meters above the basilica floor offers impressive views: Bernini's baldacchino, which is as tall as a building, looks to be a small scale model.

The last part of the climb goes between the two superimposed round vaults which make up the dome, which curve little by little as they rise to the top. A circular balcony from the lantern looks out onto the unforgettable panorama of the Eternal City.

Aerial view of the St. Peter's Square

INDEX